DARING WOMEN

25 WOMEN WHO DEFIED LIMITATIONS

by Emma Carlson Berne

COMPASS POINT BOOKS
a capstone imprint

Daring Women is published by Compass Point Books, an imprint of Capstone.
1710 Roe Crest Drive
North Mankato, Minnesota 56003
www.capstonepub.com

Library of Congress Cataloging-in-Publication Data is available on the Library of Congress website.
ISBN: 978-0-7565-6616-6 (hardcover)
ISBN: 978-0-7565-6660-9 (paperback)
ISBN: 978-0-7565-6624-1 (ebook PDF)

Summary: Discover 25 women whose disabilities did not stand in the way of their great achievements. Each woman profiled in this collection faced the challenge of a disability while pursuing excellence in her field, including the arts, sports, leadership, and sciences.

Image Credits
AP Photo: Damian Dovarganes, 50; Bob Langrish Equestrian Photographer: Bob Langrish, 23; Getty Images: AFP, 9, AFP/Jewel SAMAD, 27, Alexandre Loureiro, 32, Bettmann, 7, 35, Chip Somodevilla, 40, David M. Benett, 14, David Madison, 25, Gregory Rec/Portland Press Herald, 49, Joe Raedle, 43, Jordan Strauss, 21, Laurence Griffiths, 11, Michael Bezjian, 31, PA Images/A. Ham, 28, RJ Sangosti/The Denver Post, 19, Robert Sherbow/The LIFE Images Collection, 45, Science & Society Picture Library, 10, Sean M. Haffey, Cover; Jane Kihungi: 39; Jesse Shanahan: photo by Tim Coburn, 54; Shutterstock: Brian A. Witkin, 29, Kathy Hutchins, 47, MikeDotta, 5, s_bukley, 13; Thomas Ondrasek: 52; Wikimedia: Executive Office of the President of the United States, 41, Laura Page, 16, Stella Young, 17, U.S. Congress, restored by Adam Cuerden, 38

Editorial Credits
Editor: Kristen Mohn; Designer: Bobbie Nuytten; Media Researcher: Tracy Cummins; Production Specialist: Laura Manthe

Consultant Credit
Lisa A. Crayton, sensitivity reader

Printed in the United States of America.
PA117

TABLE OF CONTENTS

INTRODUCTION

There are many ways to achieve greatness. Inventors and athletes, teachers and advocates, performers and lawmakers—whatever the field, it takes strength and perseverance to make your mark. But historically, women have not always been allowed or encouraged to do this. Women with disabilities or limitations may not have had the resources they needed to reach their potential. And yet, women have risen to the challenge. Women with limitations have earned Oscars and Grammys. They've won Olympic races and surfed big waves. They've spearheaded movements for justice and developed scientific breakthroughs. Some are visually impaired. Some have intellectual disabilities. Some use a wheelchair. These women have worked for their achievements and have helped pave the way for others. Their achievements can inspire us to change our world as well.

> *I think the main problem we face is the tendency to see disability as a single-issue struggle, which it is not. Disabled people are a diverse group of individuals with different backgrounds and identities and they are a part of every single aspect of each society.*
>
> —Freyja Haraldsdóttir, Icelandic disability-rights activist

*Athletes with physical limitations compete in
every imaginable sport, sometimes with the aid
of special equipment.*

Chapter 1

ARTISTIC ACHIEVEMENTS

Women who create art, music, or dance make their living expressing themselves. They bring their life to their art. For women with disabilities, that sometimes includes speaking up and speaking out about what it's like to live with a limitation. Their artistry is informed by their disability, not defined by it. Our world is better and more beautiful because of artists who are willing to share their talent and passion.

Frida Kahlo
(1907–1954)

Frida Kahlo was one of the world's most famous women artists of the 1900s, yet she spent most of her adult life in pain. Kahlo endured more than 30 surgeries, and she used a wheelchair during the last years of her life. But Kahlo found inspiration in her pain and limitations rather than letting them beat her down.

Kahlo was born into a middle-class family in Coyoacán, Mexico. In 1925, when she was 18, she was in a horrific bus and streetcar accident that left her with a permanently injured leg, pelvis, and spine. She was immobilized in a body cast during her long recovery. Some scholars believe that Kahlo's desire to create art stemmed from her need to express how much pain

Frida Kahlo, 1944

she was in during her life—in a sense, the accident made her an artist.

Kahlo found her artistic and life partner when she married the well-known Mexican painter Diego Rivera in 1929. Lifelong members of the Communist Party, Kahlo and Rivera were intensely political. They traveled the world together while Rivera painted works inspired by his political beliefs and Kahlo painted deeply personal pictures. They eventually settled in Kahlo's childhood home, Blue House.

There Kahlo produced striking, sometimes disturbing, paintings that depicted her disabled body and the pain she continued to endure. She often had to wear body casts and braces to support her injured spine and leg. Kahlo would decorate and paint on the casts, using them as another canvas. At the end of her life, Kahlo was limited to her bed and wheelchair because her leg had been amputated. But she continued her artistic and political work, hosting the first exhibition of her art in Mexico while lying in her four-poster bed.

Kahlo died at age 47 on July 13, 1954, leaving behind a legacy of fierce artistic expression.

Sudha Chandran
(1965–)

The actor Sudha Chandran is sometimes called "the woman who dances on the Jaipur Foot." The Jaipur Foot is the prosthetic leg Chandran uses because of an injury from a traffic accident.

Chandran was born in the region of southern India called Kerala. She began studying traditional dance when she was only 3 years old. It was the beginning of a lifelong passion. She danced every day after school, often until late in the evening.

In 1981, Chandran was in a bus accident that fractured her right leg and caused a few cuts. Ordinarily, this would be a relatively minor injury, but Chandran's cuts were not properly cleaned by the medical staff that tended to her. The cuts became infected, and Chandran's leg developed gangrene. Her lower leg was amputated to save her life.

Chandra recuperated for six months in the hospital. She was fitted with a painful and poorly made artificial lower leg. Nonetheless, she learned to stand and to walk straight.

But when Chandran left the hospital, she heard of a different prosthetic—the "Jaipur Foot." This simple artificial leg and foot was a revolutionary invention—people all over India could afford it, it was comfortable, and it worked. Chandran was fitted for her Jaipur Foot. She had three more years of physical therapy.

Chandran burned with the desire to dance again. After more than two years of hard work, she did. Chandran performed at India's St. Xavier College to a sold-out audience. She received a standing ovation. From there, she went on to appear in countless movies and dance performances

Sudha Chandran on stage in 2010

THE JAIPUR FOOT

The Jaipur Foot was named after the city in which it was invented. It revolutionized the world of prosthetic limbs when it was designed by surgeon Pramod Karan Sethi and craftsman Pandit Ram Chandra Sharma in 1968. It was simple, without too many parts that could break, and it was made of rubber, wood, and plastic rather than carbon fiber. This made it very inexpensive. It cost just $45 to make, which made it affordable for people around the world. The Jaipur Foot was flexible, which made it comfortable, and it could be used without shoes.

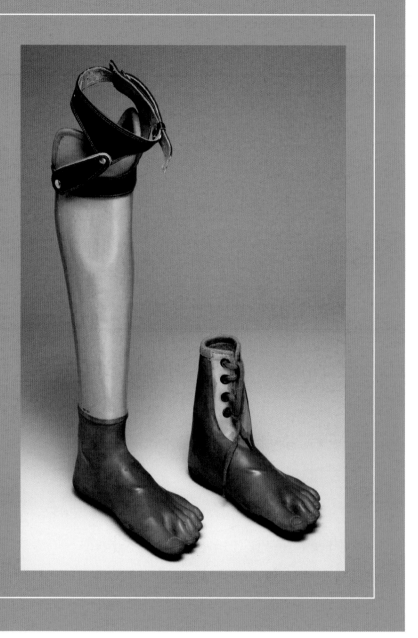

in India. She founded the Sudha Chandran School of Dance and is the vice-chairperson of India's National Association of Disabled Enterprises. She still wears her Jaipur Foot—and she still dances.

Evelyn Glennie
(1965–)

Does a musician need to be able to hear? Evelyn Glennie would answer an emphatic "No!" to that question. Glennie has a

Evelyn Glennie performed at the opening ceremony of the 2012 Olympic Games.

hearing impairment. She began losing her hearing at age 8 from nerve damage, and by age 12 she was almost completely Deaf.

But Glennie was also deeply, innately, a musician. As a child in Aberdeen, Scotland, Glennie played the piano and the clarinet. But when her hearing loss was nearly complete, she became a percussionist.

Percussionists use instruments that are beaten, shaken, rattled, or scraped. Glennie found that she could feel the vibrations of the drums and other instruments, which helped her sense their sound. "I would stand with my hands against the classroom wall while [my teacher] played notes on the timpani," Glennie wrote in a 2015 essay. "Eventually I managed to distinguish the rough pitch of notes by associating where on my body I felt the sound. . . . The low sounds I feel mainly in my legs and feet and high sounds might be particular places on my face, neck, and chest." Glennie learned to place her fingers on the edges of instruments to "hear" their pitch and to perform barefoot so she can sense vibrations through her feet. By the time she was 16, Glennie was accomplished enough to be accepted into the Royal Academy of Music.

After graduating, Glennie became the world's only full-time solo percussionist. She has played during the opening ceremony of the 2012 London Olympics, won two Grammys, released more than 30 CDs, and been the subject of the documentary *Touch the Sound*. In 1993, she received a British honor called Officer of the Order of the British Empire (OBE), which gives Glennie the title "Dame." Glennie has never stopped creating music and continues to compose and perform all over the world.

Marlee Matlin
(1965–)

Born in Illinois, actor Marlee Matlin lost most of her hearing when she was 18 months old, possibly due to a malformed cochlea. At age 21, she won an Academy Award for her role in the movie *Children of a Lesser God*, making her the first Deaf actor to bring home an Oscar.

From a young age, Matlin loved being on the stage. Her first acting experience was at age 7 in a children's theater production of *The Wizard of Oz*. As an adult, Matlin performed in stage plays in Chicago and other parts of the Midwest, including the stage version of the film that would bring her fame. In the movie version of *Children of a Lesser God,* Matlin played a frustrated Deaf girl, and her performance earned her a Golden Globe Award as well as an Oscar. At 21, she was not only the first Deaf actor but also the youngest person at the time to receive film acting's top award.

Marlee Matlin was inducted into the Hollywood Walk of Fame in 2009.

In a later interview, Matlin remembers standing onstage at the Oscar ceremony. "[My mentor] . . . told me to follow my heart and never let barriers stop me from achieving my dreams when I asked him if I could be an actor in Hollywood. . . . Dreams do come true."

Matlin has appeared in numerous other movies and TV shows. She works for the rights of the hearing-impaired as well. She has taken part in the effort to pass congressional legislation to require all TVs, broadband, and internet to contain closed-captioning technology. She has written children's books about deafness and signed in American Sign Language for high-profile public events. Matlin is aware of the power she holds by being a famous Deaf person—and she uses that power to better the lives of hearing-impaired people everywhere.

Sarah Gordy at an event for Elle *magazine in 2019*

Sarah Gordy
(1976–)

"Some people look at a person with a disability and don't see the person, just a condition." Actor Sarah Gordy spoke these words when referring to her role in the play *Jellyfish*, which centers around a girl with an intellectual disability. But she also could be referring to her own experiences.

Born and raised in the United States and England, Gordy has Down syndrome, a condition that causes developmental delay and intellectual disability. Her parents were oil engineers. Gordy's mother, Jane, found that Gordy understood concepts better if they were part of a story. Gordy and her sister would make costumes and put on plays for the family. Gordy soon found that she had real acting talent. She acted in school plays, and at age 11 she was cast in her first television show.

Since then, Gordy has appeared in numerous TV shows in the United States and England, as well as onstage. In 2018, Gordy received a Member of the Most Excellent Order of the British Empire (MBE). This honor is given by the queen of England to those who have made great achievements in the arts, among other things. Gordy was the first woman with Down syndrome to receive this award. Gordy also studied law at Nottingham University in England and became the first person with Down syndrome to receive an honorary degree from a United Kingdom university.

Gordy needs a bit longer to learn her lines than a typical actor, but otherwise she is the same as actors without disabilities. Gordy told an interviewer from *The Stage* magazine, "Down syndrome is not a different universe. We are part of this one."

Jess Thom
(1980–)

"It is the hippies of outrageous fortune that weigh heavy on the minds of dogs." This strange sentence is something Jess Thom randomly said one day. Thom has Tourette's syndrome, a neurological condition characterized by tics, which are involuntary speech or movements. The tics make Thom say any word in her vocabulary at any time. In particular, she says "biscuit" up to 16,000 times a day. Thom's movement tics also involve hitting herself repeatedly in the chest with her fist, so she wears padded gloves to protect her chest and knuckles. She often uses a wheelchair because her movements, including walking, can be unpredictable and difficult to control. Thom can't control her tics or stop them. But she can accept them.

Born in London in 1980, Thom started having tics when she was around age 6. As she grew into her 20s, the tics started

Touretteshero cofounder Jess Thom

Thom was asked by the house staff to sit in the sound booth so her tics wouldn't disturb other people. Thom felt shut out of the arts community she loved.

"Where's the one seat in the house where I'm not going to be asked to leave?" she asked herself later. The answer was obvious: on the stage itself.

Thom began addressing her Tourette's head-on by dressing up as a superhero she called Touretteshero and performing at festivals. She created the Touretteshero website and blog, and in 2013 Thom began performing in her own show, *Adventures in Biscuit Land*. "Different kinds of bodies and minds need to be visible and given equal importance," Thom said. "That's the sort of artistic community I want to be part of."

becoming more frequent. She received a diagnosis of Tourette's. Thom was always passionate about the arts. But one evening while she was attending a performance,

People who have Tourette's might have motor tics, which can include hitting themselves, jerking, twitching, or hopping, or they might have vocal tics, such as shouting words, grunting, or hooting. Some, like Jess Thom, have both.

Stella Young
(1982–2014)

Journalist and comedian Stella Young didn't want to be an inspiration. She wanted to be a person. "We've been sold this lie that disability makes you exceptional and it honestly doesn't," Young said during a talk. It just makes you a human, like every other human, she meant. Young believed that people with disabilities are capable of great contributions and small ones. They don't need to be treated as if performing regular daily tasks is a great accomplishment.

Young was born in Western Victoria, Australia, with osteogenesis imperfecta, a disease that causes bones to break very easily. It is sometimes called "brittle bone disease." Young used a wheelchair from an early age, and at 14 she conducted a test to determine which shops on her town's main street were wheelchair accessible.

Young studied education before she

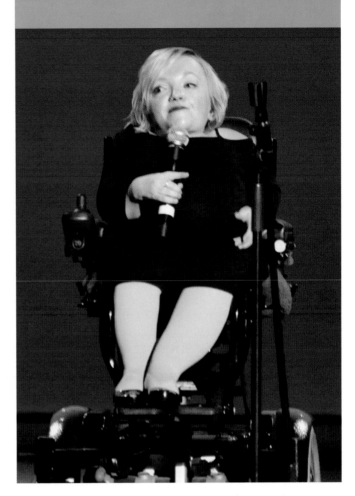

Stella Young performing at a conference in Melbourne, Australia, in 2012

became a journalist. She later went on to become a disability-rights activist, comedian, writer, and editor. She embraced the term "crip," short for "cripple," saying that she found the term empowering rather than offensive. She pointed out that the main problem of her life was not that she frequently broke her bones, but that she couldn't get her wheelchair into most buildings she wanted to enter. She didn't want sympathy or praise from the world—she wanted real-life solutions to problems that people with disabilities face every day.

Young died suddenly in 2014 at age 32 in Melbourne, Australia. To the many admirers who insisted on calling her exceptional, she said, "Disability doesn't make you exceptional, but questioning what you think you know about it does."

Prudence Mabhena
(1989–)

Prudence Mabhena's Afro-fusion band is called Liyana, which means "It's raining" in Shona, the main language in Zimbabwe. And in Zimbabwe, where Mabhena is from, rain is a blessing. So saying "It's raining" is like saying "I am blessed."

Mabhena was born in Zimbabwe with a physical disability. She has arthrogryposis, a condition in which the joints of her body do not function well. Mabhena lost both of her legs and has only limited use of her arms.

Children in Zimbabwe with disabilities often experience prejudice, neglect, and discrimination. Disabilities can be seen as a sign of witchcraft or curses. Mabhena's parents abandoned her at birth. She was raised by her grandmother, a farmer who brought Mabhena to the fields each day. She sang to Mabhena as she worked.

Soon Mabhena was singing on her own. She sang in church and in the hallways of her school, the King George VI School for the Disabled in Zimbabwe. She joined the school choir. At age 16, as a class project, Mabhena and her friends formed the band Liyana, whose members all have physical disabilities.

Since then, Liyana has toured Europe and the United States and put out two CDs. In 2010, a documentary about Mabhena's life, *Music by Prudence*, won an Oscar for Best Documentary Short Subject. In

Prudence Mabhena was profiled by the Denver Post *newspaper in 2011.*

2011 Mabhena was appointed a UNICEF National Ambassador for Zimbabwe. That same year she had spine surgery in Denver, Colorado, so that she could sit up straight in her wheelchair. Now Mabhena teaches music at King George VI School—the same place that gave rise to Liyana and to Mabhena's remarkable voice.

Chapter 2

STRENGTH IN SPORTS

Sprinters, surfers, wheelchair racers, swimmers—these are women who have defied limitations in sports. They've shown us that by harnessing their grit, determination, strength, and focus, they can do anything. They can power through the pool with prosthetic legs. They can sprint down a track—and win—even though they are legally blind. They can hear the roar of the crowd from the winners' podium—and then turn around the next day and start training again.

Loretta Claiborne
(1953–)

When Loretta Claiborne's mother was pregnant with her, she fell down a flight of stairs. As a result of that fall, Claiborne was born with a visual impairment and an intellectual disability.

Claiborne's six brothers and sisters and her mother formed a strong, loving family around Claiborne in their York, Pennsylvania, home. But Claiborne didn't walk or talk until she was 4 years old. The standard recommendation for intellectually disabled children during the 1950s was to

Loretta Claiborne spoke at a Special Olympics press conference.

put them in an institution. But Claiborne's mother refused.

She wanted her daughter to be raised the same as her other children, to just be herself. But Claiborne was constantly teased and bullied because of her disability. Kids called her rude names. So Claiborne fought back—with her fists. She felt angry and helpless. She wanted to use her words to defend herself, as her mother encouraged her to do, but it was difficult.

At home, though, Claiborne was a typical kid. She and her brother Hank would have friendly footraces together. When Claiborne was about 13, she discovered her love of running and movement. She started karate and became a fourth-degree black belt. When she was 18, she got involved in the Special Olympics— and that organization helped Claiborne find her passion.

Claiborne became a serious Special Olympics competitor. She finished 26 marathons. At the Boston Marathon, she placed twice in the top 100 female finishers.

In 1996, Claiborne's tremendous athletic talent and persistence earned her the Arthur Ashe Award for Courage—an award given to people who show strength in the face of difficulty. In 2000, Claiborne was inducted into the Women in Sports Hall of Fame. She gave speeches and met presidents. She spoke to schoolchildren regularly. Claiborne found her voice in a pair of running shoes, and she's still running.

Wendy Fryke
(1964–)

Wendy Fryke didn't think of herself as an athlete until she started riding horses competitively. Fryke was born in Parker, Colorado, in 1964 with spastic cerebral palsy. This condition makes the muscles on the right side of her body tense and unable to release. Fryke had loved horses since she was a little girl, but because cerebral palsy affected her muscle strength and balance, her parents thought riding was too

*Wendy Fryke in the ring with her horse Lateran
at the World Equestrian Games in 2010*

dangerous. A couple of trail rides was all the riding Fryke did until she was in her 30s. That was when she took a trail ride in Colorado and came home determined to enter competitive horseback riding.

Together, Fryke and her horse compete in Paralympic dressage events. In this type of "horse ballet," the horse and rider perform complex and precise moves. The horse and rider must be perfectly balanced.

Horseback riders with disabilities use a variety of adaptive equipment, such as mounting ramps, saddles with wider or deeper seats, and hoods over their stirrups.

This precision is a challenge for Fryke, whose right side is weaker and tighter than her left. Fryke uses magnetic stirrups with a hood to keep her feet from slipping. The stirrups match up with magnetic components on the bottom of her boots. She also has a special saddle that helps her balance. And to help her communicate with her horse through the bridle, Fryke uses special reins.

Fryke has ridden several horses during her career. With her mare Katanga, Fryke rode in the 2009 United States Equestrian Federation's (USEF's) Para-Equestrian Dressage National Championships. In 2010, with her stallion Lateran, Fryke won her division at an international para-equestrian competition, and she rode in the World Equestrian Games in Kentucky. Fryke also competes against people without disabilities in dressage competitions at the USEF national level.

People who have received a cerebral palsy diagnosis have to accept who they are, Fryke believes. And in Fryke's words, "Just get on with it."

Marla Runyan
(1969–)

Runner Marla Runyan can flex like a dandelion in the wind. Runyan was born on January 4, 1969, in Santa Maria, California. In elementary school she was diagnosed with Stargardt disease, which is progressive and incurable. People can develop what looks to them like a large, hazy, gray or black hole in the middle of their vision. Some people, like Runyan, may maintain sight in their peripheral vision. Runyan is also able to see some shapes and colors.

Still, Runyan barreled through childhood sports. She told *Runner's World* magazine,

Marla Runyan in the 1,500-meter preliminary event at the 1999 World Championships in Athletics

"My response was like, 'Oh, it's not a big deal . . . .'" She began running track in high school. In 1992 and 1996, she made it to the Paralympics—the Olympic-style games for athletes with disabilities—and brought home five gold medals.

But Runyan wanted the Olympics too. When she failed to qualify as a sprinter, she started training as a middle-distance runner. In 2000, Runyan qualified for the U.S. Olympic team, making her the only visually impaired American to compete in both the Paralympics and the Olympics. Runyan listened to the announcer's calls to know what lap she was on and what her time was. Runyan placed eighth in the 1,500-meter event.

In 2002, Runyan moved to marathoning. Her vision was getting progressively worse. Runyan could see only about 15 feet (4.6 meters) in front of her. But in 2002, Runyan ran the New York City marathon in 2 hours, 27 minutes, 10 seconds, making her the fourth-fastest debut American marathoner in history at the time. In 2004, she made the U.S. Olympic team for the second time and ran the 5,000 meters at the Athens Games.

"I kind of believed that if I worked hard enough, I could overcome anything," Runyan said in an interview. "I was going to figure anything out."

Zahra Nemati
(1985–)

Zahra Nemati was born in Iran in 1985. By the time she was a university student, she had earned a black belt in the martial art tae kwon do. She was on the Iranian national team and had her sights set on the Olympics. Then in 2004, at age 18, Nemati was hit by a car. Her spine was severed and she was paralyzed from the waist down. She would need to use a wheelchair.

Nemati's resilience and optimism helped her recover. In 2007, Nemati became an athlete again. She took up archery. The sport both made her strong and taught her the meaning of strength, Nemati said. She had been given another chance to live after her accident. But she needed mental and emotional, as well as physical, strength.

Only six months after starting archery training, Nemati competed in Iran's national archery championships. She took third place and was invited to join the Iranian Paralympic archery team.

Five years after that, Nemati found herself competing against other athletes at the 2012 London Paralympic Games. She won gold—the first Iranian woman to win a gold medal at the Olympics or Paralympics.

Nemati wasn't done yet. In 2015, she took silver in the Asian Archery Championships in Bangkok. That was a qualifier for the Olympics. Nemati was going to experience the Olympic dreams that she'd thought were lost after her accident 11 years earlier.

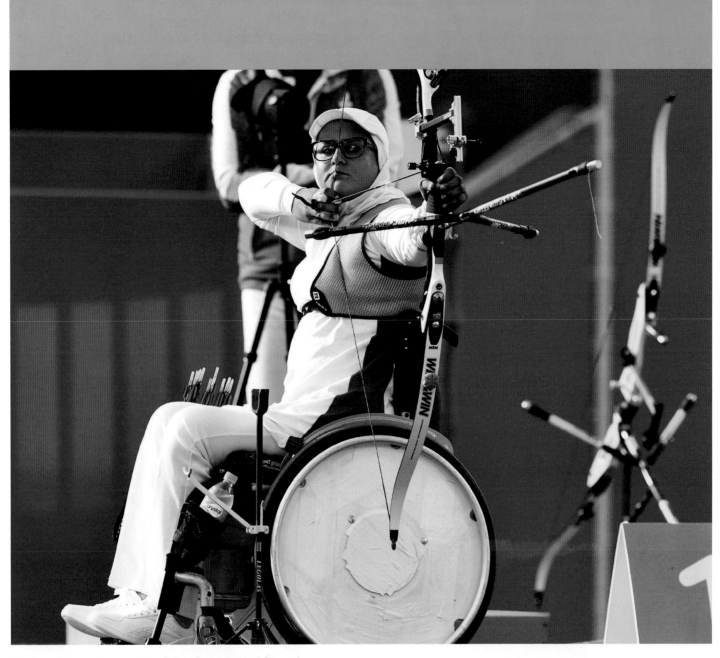

Zahra Nemati competed in the 2016 Olympics in Rio de Janeiro, Brazil.

The next year, in 2016, Nemati went to the Olympics in Rio de Janeiro. She traveled with Iran's national team to compete against athletes without disabilities, and she was their flag bearer in the opening ceremony. Nemati shot her very best, coming in 33rd in the field. "Don't let your disability defeat you," she said. It certainly has never defeated Nemati.

THE HISTORY OF THE PARALYMPICS

In the 1940s, physician Ludwig Guttmann was treating World War II veterans at the National Spinal Injuries Centre in England. He noticed that veterans with spinal injuries became depressed and out of shape. Guttmann conceived of the Paralympics—the Olympic-style games for athletes with physical disabilities. The first Paralympics were held in 1948 at the Stoke Mandeville Hospital near Oxford, England. Archery was the only sport featured so that patients could use their upper-body strength. During this era, patients with spinal injuries were considered useless and hopeless. The games showed otherwise. By 1953, seven sports were included, and 3,000 people watched 200 athletes from eight countries compete. The Paralympics have taken place every four years since.

Stoke Mandeville Paralympics, 1957

Bethany Hamilton
(1990–)

Bethany Hamilton loves the water. Born on the Hawaiian island of Kauai, she started surfing when she was 7 years old. She won her first surf competition at age 8, and by the time she was 9, Hamilton had signed sponsorship deals. She was ready for a surf career.

But Hamilton's life changed forever on October 31, 2003. She was surfing with her best friend at legendary Hawaiian surf spot Tunnels Beach when she was attacked in calm waters by a 14-foot (4.3-m) tiger shark. The shark bit off Hamilton's arm just below the shoulder. Hamilton's friend's father made a bandage out of his T-shirt and a tourniquet out of his surf leash, saving her life, but Hamilton lost more than 60 percent of her blood.

Bethany Hamilton surfed at the 2013 Supergirl Surf Pro competition in Oceanside, California.

Hamilton began talking about returning to surfing while still in her hospital room— and one month later she did. Surfing is about nerve and balance; Hamilton had plenty of nerve, but she had to relearn to balance without her arm. She found she had to paddle just as fast as she used to if she hoped to compete at the highest levels of professional surfing.

Hamilton found ways to adapt. She began using a shorter surfboard equipped with a handle at the front that helped her during paddle-outs. Then, less than two years after her accident, Hamilton won her first national surfing title. She became a professional surfer, an author, a speaker, and the subject of a 2011 movie, *Soul Surfer*, that highlighted her grit and determination. In 2016, Hamilton beat out a six-time world champion as well as the top-ranked female surfer in the world when she finished third at the World Surf League's Fiji Women's Pro competition. "I don't need easy," Hamilton wrote. "I just need possible."

Chelsea Werner
(1993–)

"Everyone has challenges in their lives, but it's how you deal with those challenges that makes all the difference," Chelsea Werner said in an interview. She has lived up to those words.

A gymnast and a model, Werner is also a person with Down syndrome. Down syndrome is a genetic condition that can affect a person's muscle tone, intellectual ability, and development. When Werner was born, doctors told her parents that she would always have low muscle tone. Werner didn't walk until she was almost 2. Athletics would be hard.

And they were. When Werner began gymnastics at age 8, she had all the enthusiasm in the world. But her low muscle tone made it difficult for her just to walk on a balance beam. Her coach, Dawn Pombo, didn't let Werner off the hook, though. Instead, she made Werner practice

Chelsea Werner at a modeling shoot in Los Angeles in 2018

over and over, breaking down the moves into tiny steps.

Pombo's coaching, combined with Werner's immense desire to push herself, worked. Werner won the Special Olympics National Championship in gymnastics four times. She has said that the floor routine is her favorite event.

Werner thought of herself as a gymnast, but when the clothing company Aerie started an ad campaign highlighting diversity and inclusion, the company selected Werner as a model, saying that she was strong, proud, and beautiful. Soon after, Werner signed with the fashion agency We Speak. She began modeling for the clothing company H&M, appeared on the cover of *Teen Vogue* magazine, and walked the runway at New York's Fashion Week.

Her life in front of the camera has helped Werner to see herself as a role model for other people with disabilities: "If I can help give anyone hope, that makes me very happy and proud!"

*Chelsea McClammer competing at the 2016
Rio de Janeiro Paralympics*

Chelsea McClammer

(1994–)

Wheelchair track athlete Chelsea McClammer doesn't remember much of her life before the car accident that paralyzed her at age 6. McClammer was born in Washington State in 1994. On the day her life changed forever, she was riding in the back seat of the family car with her mother and brother. An oncoming car struck theirs.

When McClammer woke up in the hospital, doctors told her that she was paralyzed.

But McClammer has said that because she was so young, the adjustment was not so hard. When she returned to kindergarten, she was determined to build up enough strength to play on the monkey bars like the other kids. And she did.

McClammer has been an athlete her entire life, and her wheelchair is more a partner than an impediment. With her chair, she played basketball, tennis, and track growing up. At the age of 11, at a sports convention, she learned about wheelchair racing. "I never saw anything like it before," McClammer said. "The first time I did it . . . it felt like the coolest thing ever, and it still is to me."

By the time she was 14, McClammer was the youngest member of the 2008 Paralympic U.S. Track and Field team in Beijing. She didn't win a medal in those games, but eight years later, she was back at the 2016 Paralympic Games in Rio de Janeiro. She took home two silver medals and a bronze.

Off the track, McClammer hopes to be a rehabilitation counselor for children with disabilities one day. She'd like to help kids who are in the same position she once was. McClammer makes it clear that she does not feel oppressed by her disability. Just the opposite, in fact. Without her chair, she'd never have achieved what she has.

> **I never saw anything like it before. The first time I did it . . . it felt like the coolest thing ever, and it still is to me.**
> —Chelsea McClammer

Chapter 3

ACTIVISTS WORKING FOR CHANGE

Leaders and activists refuse to hide. Whether these women were born with disabilities or their lives were changed forever by accidents or disease, they have brought themselves out into the open and insisted that work for others with disabilities get done. They've passed laws, they've made speeches, and they've written books. They've demanded that people acknowledge them—with their limitations—and all people with disabilities.

Helen Keller
(1880–1968)

No one thought that Helen Keller would ever learn to communicate. Born in Alabama, she was a lively, active little girl until 19 months old, when she came down with an illness that may have been scarlet fever. Keller recovered eventually—but she was left both blind and Deaf.

Keller's family didn't know how to help her. Keller ran wild and had terrible tantrums because she was so frustrated about not being able to communicate.

Helen Keller, 1950s

Keller's life changed forever in 1887, at age 7, when the woman who would become her lifelong teacher, friend, and companion arrived at the Keller house: Annie Sullivan.

Sullivan taught Keller how to communicate by using the manual alphabet—a system of signing into people's hands and allowing them to sign into her hands. Sullivan taught Keller to read braille.

Keller had a quick mind and a bold personality. With Sullivan at her side, Keller attended Radcliffe College—the women's

IN KELLER'S OWN WORDS

In her memoir, *The Story of My Life*, Helen Keller wrote movingly of the first moment when she connected words and objects, with the help of her teacher, Annie Sullivan:

We walked down the path to the well-house, attracted by the fragrance of the honeysuckle with which it was covered. Someone was drawing water and my teacher [Annie Sullivan] placed my hand under the spout. As the cool stream gushed over one hand she spelled into the other the word water, first slowly, then rapidly. I stood still, my whole attention fixed upon the motions of her fingers. Suddenly I felt a misty consciousness as of something forgotten—a thrill of returning thought; and somehow the mystery of language was revealed to me. I knew then that "w-a-t-e-r" meant the wonderful cool something that was flowing over my hand. That living word awakened my soul, gave it light, hope, joy, set it free! There were barriers still, it is true, but barriers that could in time be swept away.

college of Harvard University. In 1904, Keller became the first deaf-blind person ever to graduate from college.

She loved interacting with people, and she was good at it. She and Sullivan were popular lecturers. At one point, Keller and Sullivan performed in vaudeville shows onstage. They would demonstrate how Keller communicated. Keller wrote numerous books, including two memoirs describing how she saw the world. She worked on behalf of civil rights and supported veterans blinded in World War II.

Keller lived a long life, outliving both Sullivan and the companion that followed her, Polly Thomson. Polly's successor, Winifred Corbally, was at Keller's bedside when Keller passed away in her sleep at age 87. Keller had spent her life achieving a series of staggering firsts for women with disabilities and left behind a powerful legacy.

Barbara Jordan
(1936–1996)

Barbara Jordan was born in 1936 in Houston, Texas. Her family didn't have much money, but they did value education. Her father was a Baptist minister who took shifts as a warehouse clerk so that he could pay for her college. Jordan would go on to spend decades in public service while dealing with multiple sclerosis, a central nervous system disease that can affect balance and mobility.

Jordan and her sisters attended the segregated schools of Houston, where Jordan was a brilliant debater and student. When she attended Boston University's law school, she was one of only a few black students in the program.

Jordan became a lawyer and a civil rights activist. She campaigned for John F. Kennedy's presidential bid before entering politics herself and winning a seat in the Texas state legislature as its first black

Barbara Jordan's portrait published in Black Americans in Congress, 1870–2007

representative in 1966. In 1972, she was elected to the U.S. House of Representatives, the first black person from Texas to have been elected since Reconstruction.

In 1979, Jordan did not run for a fourth term in Congress. It was around this time that she was diagnosed with multiple sclerosis. Jordan preferred to keep her disease private and rarely spoke about it in public. She taught for 17 years at the Lyndon B. Johnson School of Public Affairs at the University of Texas. In 1992, Jordan gave a speech at the Democratic National Convention.

Jordan died at age 59 from pneumonia that was a result of leukemia. Her work as a pioneering legislator and stateswoman lives on.

Jane Kihungi
(1962-)

"Society has been more disabling than the impairment itself," Jane Kihungi said. Born in Kenya, Kihungi caught the polio virus in 1967 when she was 5 years old. Her right side and arm were paralyzed. In Kenya at the time, people with disabilities were looked down on. Kihungi's parents wanted to protect her from this stigma. At first they kept her home, sending her younger brother to school instead. When they did send Kihungi to school, she was teased and bullied.

Kihungi always had the support of her family, who never treated her differently than her siblings. Kihungi eventually graduated from college, studying community development. She wanted to help other women with disabilities in Kenya—women who were facing challenges that men with disabilities did not face. Kihungi and eight other women

Jane Kihungi, cofounder of Women Challenged to Challenge

started Women Challenged to Challenge (WCC), an organization of women with disabilities. When the women speak out as a group, Kihungi explains, their voices are more powerful than when they speak alone. They can attract the attention of the government and can advocate for programs that they need.

In 2000, the WCC founders began meeting in each other's homes and raising money. The government granted the group land for a workspace but they had no money for a building, so they bought a small shipping container to use as an office.

Gradually, WCC grew to have 1,300 members. In 2014, the group did a research study that revealed that women and girls with disabilities were not represented enough in all areas of government and leadership. In 2017, the group ran an education campaign that reached women with disabilities all over Kenya. The goal was to educate them about voting and the electoral process. Because of Kihungi's determination, women with disabilities in Kenya now have a powerful voice speaking just for them.

Tammy Duckworth
(1968–)

Losing both her legs in combat in Iraq affected the course of Illinois senator Tammy Duckworth's life and career. Duckworth was born in 1968 to a Thai mother and an American father. The family

Tammy Duckworth served in the U.S. House of Representatives for four years before becoming a U.S. senator in 2017.

went through periods of poverty while Duckworth was growing up. At one point, she sold flowers by the side of the road to make money for her family.

Duckworth joined the Illinois Army National Guard and, in 2004, deployed to Iraq as a pilot flying the advanced Blackhawk military helicopters. On

President George H.W. Bush signed the Americans with Disabilities Act.

In 1990, Congress passed the Americans with Disabilities Act (ADA). It was the first comprehensive civil rights legislation specifically aimed at people with disabilities.

November 12, her helicopter was hit by a rocket-propelled grenade. Duckworth almost died. Both of her legs had to be amputated, and she lost some use of her right arm.

But just eight weeks after her surgery, Duckworth was invited to President George W. Bush's State of the Union address. Attendees were impressed with her determination. Duckworth began advocating for veterans. In 2009, President Barack Obama appointed her Assistant Secretary of Veterans Affairs. In 2012, Duckworth was elected to the House of Representatives and served two terms before she was elected to the Senate in 2016.

Duckworth uses titanium prosthetic legs and a wheelchair to get around. She also has a pair of prosthetic legs that look very real. But to Duckworth, those legs represent loss. Her metal prosthesis, she said, represents strength. She refuses to hide her wheelchair in photos. It's no different than a medal on her chest, she has said. It's something to be proud of.

Duckworth had been one of the first female army soldiers to fly combat missions in Operation Iraqi Freedom (OIF); the first female double amputee in the Senate; and the first woman to give birth while serving as a senator. Since becoming a mother, Duckworth has worked to pass legislation that supports mothers and working families.

Gabrielle Giffords
(1970-)

Gabrielle Giffords was a bright star in the U.S. House of Representatives when a bullet changed her life. Giffords was born on June 8, 1970, in Tucson, Arizona. At age 32, she became the youngest woman to be elected to the Arizona Senate. In 2007, Giffords made the leap to the U.S. Congress.

On January 8, 2011, Giffords was hosting an event she called "Congress on Your Corner." She was in the parking lot of a supermarket in Tucson. A man named Jared Lee Loughner shot her in the back of the head. He shot 19 people that day, injuring 13 and killing six. Doctors later stated that 90 percent of people with Giffords's type of brain injury die. Amazingly, she survived. But she had suffered extensive brain damage from the bullet that pierced her head. She had severe difficulty speaking and her right arm and leg were paralyzed. Her vision was damaged in both eyes.

Gabrielle (Gabby) Giffords gave a speech at the 2016 Democratic National Convention, at which Hillary Rodham Clinton was nominated the Democratic presidential candidate.

Giffords came back to Congress in August 2011. But balancing her new disabilities and her congressional work was too difficult. On January 25, 2012, Giffords resigned from Congress.

Giffords continues to face challenges from her injuries. The right side of her body remains paralyzed. She still struggles with speech. She has said that she often feels as if the words are just on the tip of her tongue, but she can't quite make them come out.

Giffords's intellect was not affected. She now runs Giffords, a gun-control organization. She has not retreated from public life but travels around the country speaking out against gun violence. The words she spoke when she resigned from the House are still true: "Every day, I am working hard. I will recover and will return, and we will work together again . . . for all Americans."

Chapter 4

LEADING IN LEARNING

Being a woman scientist, academic, or educator comes with unique challenges. Often, women in science and academics have faced discrimination for working in what were historically considered male fields. And a woman with a disability working in those fields? That can pose even greater obstacles. But these women blow those obstacles apart. They speak out— loudly—about their research, their work, and what they need to fulfill their potential. When faced with prejudice against autism, physical limitations, or mental illness, they demand that their detractors step aside. Then they get on with their work.

Kay Redfield Jamison
(1946–)

"To suffer is to have learned," Kay Redfield Jamison told an audience of fellow doctors and researchers. Jamison has long struggled with bipolar disorder, which she feels is more accurately called *manic-depressive illness*. Bipolar disorder is a

Kay Redfield Jamison, 1993

mental illness that involves shifts in energy and activity, often involving periods of "highs" (mania) and "lows" (depression). Medication can help control the symptoms of bipolar disorder, but there is no cure. People have this condition throughout their life.

Jamison was diagnosed when she was in her late 20s. For many years, she hid her disordered thinking from her colleagues at the University of California, Los Angeles (UCLA), where she was an assistant professor of psychiatry. But when she was experiencing a manic episode, Jamison was unable to control her thinking or her actions. She would make wild purchases, such as buying snakebite kits because she thought God had told her there was going to be a rattlesnake infestation. When Jamison was in periods of depression, she thought of committing suicide.

Jamison took medication for bipolar disorder and after awhile, her moods stabilized. She taught and wrote, focusing on the link between mental illness and creativity. Eventually, she said she was "tired of the hypocrisy and tired of acting as though I had nothing to hide." She wrote her own story about manic-depressive illness, *An Unquiet Mind*, published in 1995, and opened up a door to mental health acceptance. To have a well-respected psychiatry professor write so personally about her own mental illness was new and startling.

Jamison began collecting awards and grants and became a respected speaker on mental illness. She still writes and teaches. Manic-depressive illness is not easy to live with, Jamison has said. She continues to speak up for those who do.

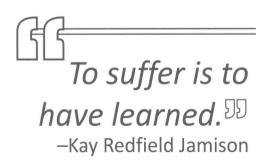

To suffer is to have learned.
—Kay Redfield Jamison

Temple Grandin

(1947–)

Temple Grandin has spent her adult life giving a voice to animals. As a professor of animal science at Colorado State University, she has pioneered humane restraint systems for animals in slaughterhouses. Thousands of animals have been spared from fear and pain during their last moments of life thanks to Grandin.

Yet Grandin herself did not speak until she was almost 4 years old. Grandin was born with autism, a condition that affects social and emotional skills, speech, and other kinds of communication. At the time, the condition was not well understood, and doctors encouraged parents to put children with disabilities like Grandin's in an institution. Grandin's mother refused. Instead, Grandin received speech therapy and learned

Temple Grandin attended the 2010 Emmy Awards, at which a movie about her life, called Temple Grandin, *won the award for Best Made for Television Movie or Miniseries.*

WHAT DOES IT FEEL LIKE TO HAVE AUTISM?

People with autism are often exquisitely sensitive to sounds, smells, and even textures. It can be hard to tune things out or ignore stimuli. Here, speaker Lori Sealy describes what autism feels like for her:

Where sound is concerned, the voices and vibrations of this world are always pounding upon me. Life is loud! This can make carrying on a conversation in a room full of people a true challenge—because I hear everything at equal volume. My auditory abilities are often extreme. In that room, I hear your hair. Yes, you read that right. In a room full of people I literally can hear when someone's hair moves in the wind or when they brush their fingers through it. In that room as you and I are trying to talk, I am hearing everyone else's conversations as clearly as our own (along with their hair). . . . As a young child I was barely able to eat in front of others . . . because of the pain I felt when someone's fork touched their teeth. In a restaurant, I was always undone because not only did I hear multiple food implements on everyone's incisors, but also all of the kitchen noise, and chewing, and swallowing, and breathing, and the transfer of change at the cash register, and the hum of the fluorescent lights, and everyone's clothes making contact with their chair . . . on and on and on it goes.

to talk. By the time she was 5, she was able to enter a typical kindergarten.

But autism made school hard for Grandin. Kids teased her because she acted and talked differently. Grandin focused on her "fixations"—intense, specific interests that many people with autism have. In Grandin's case, she was deeply connected to animals, particularly horses and cattle on her aunt's ranch, where she spent her summers. Grandin has said that she sees the world in pictures rather than words, much like animals do. This helps her better understand how an animal thinks.

Because of this deep understanding, Grandin designed a system that shields and gently squeezes cattle to keep them from becoming alarmed as they enter the slaughterhouse. Today, more than half of all the cattle slaughterhouses in the United States use humane handling equipment designed by Grandin.

Grandin had dedicated herself to autism education as well. She writes, lectures, and

"I hardly know what to say about this remarkable book.... It provides a way to understand the many kinds of sentience, human and animal, that adorn the earth."
— Elizabeth Marshall Thomas, author of *The Hidden Life of Dogs*

THINKING IN PICTURES
AND OTHER REPORTS FROM MY LIFE WITH AUTISM
TEMPLE GRANDIN
WITH A FOREWORD BY OLIVER SACKS

Temple Grandin is the author of many books about animals and life with autism.

explains the autistic mind for researchers and educators. Grandin has been adamant that those with autism are "different, not less."

Elyn Saks, a recipient of a MacArthur Foundation "genius grant," on the University of Southern California campus, where she is a professor of psychology

Elyn Saks

(1956–)

Elyn Saks is a professor, an author, and a person who lives with a serious mental illness—schizophrenia. Born and raised in Miami, Saks remembers that one of her first serious episodes of schizophrenia came when she was 16. Walking home from school, she began to think that the houses were communicating secret messages to her.

Schizophrenia is a mental illness in which people often have hallucinations or delusions—they have thoughts that are out of touch with reality and see or hear things that are not real. Often, people with schizophrenia have trouble working or doing daily activities. Saks was in her 20s and studying at Oxford University in England when she began having full-blown schizophrenia with delusions and disordered thinking. She continued having psychotic episodes when she was studying at Yale Law School, including one in which she found herself singing on the roof of the library at midnight.

Saks has explained that she needed medication and treatment but that she resisted it. She felt that if she ignored her problems, they would go away. She did eventually take medication, but whenever she stopped taking the drugs, her delusions would return.

With the help of therapists, Saks eventually decided to stay on her medication, and her thoughts cleared. She refused to hide her mental illness and became a professor of law and psychiatry at the University of Southern California. In 2007, she published the groundbreaking memoir *The Center Cannot Hold*, in which she frankly and openly described life with schizophrenia. She speaks, lectures, and conducts research about schizophrenia. Most importantly, she brings hope and awareness to a subject that is often seen as shameful. Saks is not ashamed, and she is determined that other people who have schizophrenia won't be either.

Naomi Ondrasek
(1984–)

Born in Warrenton, Virginia, Naomi Ondrasek was fascinated with the natural world even as a child. She went on to study biology at Randolph-Macon Woman's College and neuroscience in graduate school at the University of California, Berkeley. She worked as a neuroscientist, studying brain chemicals and hormones.

Throughout high school, Ondrasek had gastrointestinal issues. When she turned 21, the symptoms became more severe. Just as she was starting her doctoral program, she was diagnosed with inflammatory bowel disease, a chronic condition in which the body attacks its own intestine.

Ondrasek realized that to continue her scientific work, she had to be honest with the people around her. She would gain nothing by hiding the pain and occasional embarrassment of the disease. She had to boldly ask for support from others.

Neuroscientist Naomi Ondrasek at work in her lab

She worked to educate her advisors about her condition and to convey that she would be having periods of time when she was ill. "One of the hardest things about chronic illness is the fear of uncertainty, about what your future will look like.

It takes courage . . . to keep going . . . . There will be times when you're flying, and times when you're just waiting to feel better," Ondrasek says.

Ondrasek is now a policy advisor and researcher for the Learning Policy

Institute. This group helps communicate research conclusions to lawmakers and government officials so that they can make more informed decisions about education. Ondrasek spends time thinking about what science means for people, especially kids and schools. She's helping lawmakers understand science too, so they can make good decisions for all.

Inflammatory bowel disease will never go away. But Ondrasek manages it with medications, exercise, and activities that lower her stress, like playing ukulele and spending time with her children. That way, she can continue with her scientific work. And everyone benefits when people with disabilities can do their best work.

> *There will be times when you're flying, and times when you're just waiting to feel better.*
> —Naomi Ondrasek

Jesse Shanahan
(1991–)

Data scientist Jesse Shanahan was not focused on disability accessibility when she was growing up on military bases around the country. As a kid, she was mostly focused on sports, video games, and school. She attended the University of Virginia and then went to graduate school at Wesleyan University to earn a master's degree in astronomy.

But one morning, at the age of 20, Shanahan woke up in so much pain that she couldn't turn over in bed. She spent four years going to different specialists, trying to find out what was wrong.

Eventually, she was diagnosed with Ehlers-Danlos syndrome, a genetic connective tissue disease that affects the whole body, including the joints and blood vessels. She could not climb steps without fear of a fall. She walked with a cane and had to go to physical therapy.

Jesse Shanahan, founder of the #disabledandSTEM movement

As Shanahan learned about her diagnosis, she realized just how unwelcoming the academic and scientific community could be to a person with a chronic illness or other disability. When she needed accommodations, such as extensions on assignments so she could go to therapy, she was scolded. Academic events held at buildings with many steps were difficult for her.

Science and academia had a culture problem, Shanahan realized. A scientist with a disability was not accepted.

Shanahan wanted to change this. She created the Twitter campaign #disabledandSTEM, which raises awareness of scientists and others with chronic illness, and which brings people with disabilities together. And Shanahan cofounded the Working Group on Accessibility and Disability (WGAD) in the American Astronomical Society, which promotes accessibility for scientists with disabilities, especially graduate students in astronomy. If you are a young person with a disability, Shanahan says, "Don't be afraid to do things differently. . . . No one changed the world by limiting themselves to being 'normal.'"

> *Don't be afraid to do things differently. . . . No one changed the world by limiting themselves to being 'normal.'*
> —Jesse Shanahan

Timeline

1904 Helen Keller becomes the first deaf-blind person to graduate from college.

1942 Frida Kahlo's paintings are a part of the exhibit "Twentieth Century Portraits" at the Museum of Modern Art in New York City.

1972 Barbara Jordan is elected to the U.S. House of Representatives, the first black person from Texas to have been elected since Reconstruction.

1987 Marlee Matlin receives an Academy Award for her starring role in the movie *Children of a Lesser God*.

1993 Evelyn Glennie receives the honor Officer of the Order of the British Empire (OBE) from Queen Elizabeth.

1995 Kay Redfield Jamison publishes *An Unquiet Mind*, her memoir about manic-depressive illness.

2000 Marla Runyan qualifies for the U.S. Olympic team, making her the only visually impaired American to compete in both the Paralympics and the Olympics.

Loretta Claiborne is inducted into the Women in Sports Hall of Fame.

Jane Kihungi founds Women Challenged to Challenge (WCC).

2003 Bethany Hamilton returns to surfing one month after her arm is severed in a shark attack.

2005 Prudence Mabhena and friends found their band, Liyana, as part of a class project.

2007 Elyn Saks publishes the groundbreaking memoir *The Center Cannot Hold*, in which she describes life with schizophrenia.

2008 Chelsea McClammer becomes the youngest member of the Beijing 2008 Paralympic U.S. Track and Field team.

2011 Gabrielle Giffords returns to Congress eight months after being shot in the head during an assassination attempt.

2012 Tammy Duckworth is elected to the U.S. House of Representatives.

2013 Jess Thom creates the show *Adventures in Biscuit Land*, in which she talks openly about Tourette's syndrome.

2016 Zahra Nemati travels to the Olympics with the Iranian national team to compete against athletes without disabilities.

2018 Sarah Gordy receives the honor Member of the Most Excellent Order of the British Empire (MBE), becoming the first woman with Down syndrome to receive this award.

Glossary

accessible—a place that can be entered easily

braille—a system of written language for people with visual impairment, in which raised dots formed into patterns can be felt by the fingertips

cochlea—a part of the inner ear that produces nerve impulses in reaction to sound vibrations

delusion—something that is falsely believed

developmental delay—a condition in which a child is less developed, mentally or physically, than a typical child of that age

diagnosis—the identification of a problem by examination of its symptoms

discrimination—the unjust or unfair treatment of categories of people

disordered—not functioning in a normal or healthy way

dressage—an equestrian sport in which a trained horse shows its ability to move precisely and gracefully based on cues from its rider

gangrene—a condition that occurs when flesh decays

gastrointestinal—relating to the stomach or intestine

hallucination—something seen that is not really there

humane—with sympathy and compassion

immobilize—to make unable to move

paralyzed—being unable to move

peripheral—relating to the outer part of the field of vision

prejudice—a preconceived opinion that is not based on actual experience

prosthetic—relating to an artificial body part

Reconstruction—the period of time following the Civil War (1861–1865) when the U.S. government tried to reunite the nation

resilience—ability to recover quickly from difficulties

stigma—marked by shame

tic—a muscle contraction or vocalization that a person cannot control

tourniquet—a cord or tight bandage that stops the flow of blood through a vein or artery

Critical Thinking Questions

1. On what key issues have women leaders with disabilities focused? What issue do you think is particularly important and why?
2. Do you think that the rights of those with disabilities should be protected by the federal government, as are the rights of those of different races, genders, and ethnicities? Why or why not?
3. People with disabilities sometimes face prejudice and discrimination. What are two ways that the women in these pages have combated prejudice? What is one way you could combat prejudice or discrimination in your own school or community?

Further Reading

Lawrence, Sandra. *Anthology of Amazing Women: Trailblazers Who Dared to Be Different.* New York: Little Bee Books, 2018.

Sherman, Jill. *Daring Women: 25 Women Who Fought Back.* North Mankato, MN: Capstone Press, 2019.

Skeers, Linda. *Women Who Dared: 52 Stories of Fearless Daredevils, Adventurers & Rebels.* Naperville, IL: Sourcebooks, 2017.

Internet Sites

BBC Newsround: Paralympics
http://news.bbc.co.uk/cbbcnews/hi/find_out/guides/sport/paralympics/newsid_3642000/3642508.stm

Helen Keller Kids Museum Online: Helen Keller Biography,
https://braillebug.org/helen_keller_bio.asp

KidsHealth: Kids With Special Needs
https://kidshealth.org/en/kids/special-needs.html

Source Notes

p. 4, "I think the main problem…" "Q&A with Freyja Haraldsdóttir, Icelandic Disability and Women's Rights Advocate," Election Access, November 2018, http://www.electionaccess.org/en/media/news/79/ Accessed March 3, 2020.

p. 11, "I would stand with…" "Evelyn Glennie," Polar Music Prize, Nd, https://www.polarmusicprize.org/laureates/evelyn-glennie/ Accessed October 17, 2019.

p. 13, "[My mentor]…told me…" Marlee Matlin, "Oscars: Marlee Matlin on Her Best Actress Win," *Entertainment Weekly*, February 21, 2012, https://ew.com/article/2012/02/21/oscars-marlee-matlin/ Accessed October 10, 2019.

p. 14, "Some people look…" Natasha Sutton Williams, "Sarah Gordy: 'I Wasn't Looking for a Professional Acting Career. It Found Me,'" *The Stage*, July 2, 2019, https://www.thestage.co.uk/features/interviews/2019/sarah-gordy-professional-acting-career/ Accessed October 8, 2019.

p. 15, "Down syndrome is not…" Ibid.

p. 15, "It is the hippies of…" Celia Topping, "Life Less Ordinary—Jess Thom, Disability Superhero," Tourettes Action, Nd, https://www.tourettes-action.org.uk/index.php?r=99 Accessed October 14, 2019.

p. 16, "Different kinds of bodies…" Natasha Tripney, "Touretteshero's Jess Thom: 'Disabled People Need to Be Written In, Not Out,'" *The Stage*, February 28, 2018, https://www.thestage.co.uk/features/interviews/2018/tourettesheros-jess-thom-interview-disabled-people-need-to-written-in-not-out/ Accessed October 14, 2019.

p. 17, "We've been sold this…" Elahe Izadi, "The Legacy of Stella Young, Australian Disability Advocate and Comedian," *Washington Post*, December 8, 2014, https://www.washingtonpost.com/news/arts-and-entertainment/wp/2014/12/08/the-legacy-of-stella-young-australian-disability-advocate-and-comedian/ Accessed October 18, 2019.

p. 18, "Disability doesn't make you…" Melissa Davey, "Stella Young, Disability Activist, Dies at 32," *The Guardian*, December 7, 2014, https://www.theguardian.com/australia-news/2014/dec/08/stella-young-disability-activist-dies/ Accessed October 22, 2019.

p. 24, "Just get on with it," "Wendy Fryke: 'You're Trying to Hit That Perfect Mark,'" PBS Medal Quest, Nd, http://www.pbs.org/wgbh/medal-quest/video/detail/wendy-fryke-youre-trying-hit-perfect-mark/ Accessed September 26, 2019.

p. 25, "My response was like…" Alison Wade, "Retired Pro Marla Runyan Continues to Inspire," *Runner's World,* October 1, 2014, https://www.runnersworld.com/races-places/a20820064/retired-pro-marla-runyan-continues-to-inspire/ Accessed September 23, 2019.

p. 26, "I kind of believed that…" Ibid.

p. 27, "Don't let your disability…" Helen Pidd, "Trail-Blazer Zahra Nemati Wins Hearts and Minds with Stirring Effort in Archery," *The Guardian,* August 9, 2016, https://www.theguardian.com/sport/2016/aug/09/zahra-nemati-olympics-heart-and-minds-archery Accessed October 7, 2019.

p. 30, "I don't need easy," Bethany Hamilton, "I Don't Need Easy," December 6, 2018, https://bethanyhamilton.com/%E2%80%8Bi-dont-need-easy/ Accessed October 1, 2019.

p. 30, "Everyone has challenges…" Kim Constantinesco, "Chelsea Werner, a Gymnast-Turned-Model, Is Breaking New Ground," Purpose 2 Play, Nd, https://purpose2play.com/2018/12/29/chelsea-werner-gymnast-turned-model-breaking-new-groundchelsea-werner-a-gymnast-turned-model-is-breaking-new-ground/ Accessed October 4, 2019.

p. 31, "If I can help…" Lela London, "From Special Olympian to High Fashion Model, Chelsea Werner Defies All Down Syndrome Stereotypes," *Forbes,* February 5, 2019, https://www.forbes.com/sites/lelalondon/2019/02/05/from-special-olympian-to-high-fashion-model-chelsea-werner-defies-all-down-syndrome-stereotypes/ Accessed October 4, 2019.

p. 33, "I never saw anything…" "Chelsea McClammer Biography," International Paralympic Committee, Nd, https://www.paralympic.org/chelsea-mcclammer/ Accessed September 24, 2019.

p. 36, "We walked down the path…" Helen Keller, *The Story of My Life,* 1905, https://digital.library.upenn.edu/women/keller/life/life.html Accessed October 22, 2019.

p. 39, "Society has been more…" "Empowering Kenyan Women with Disabilities as Policy Experts," International Foundation for Electoral Systems, September 11, 2018, https://www.ifes.org/news/empowering-kenyan-women-disabilities-policy-advocates Accessed October 24, 2019.

p. 43, "Every day, I am working…" "Giffords, Gabrielle," History, Art & Archives, Nd, https://history.house.gov/People/Detail/14267 Accessed October 23, 2019.

p. 44/46, "To suffer is to…" Jacqueline L. Salmon, "Kay Redfield Jamison: A Profile in Courage," BP Hope, Winter 2009, https://www.bphope.com/kay-redfield-jamison-a-profile-in-courage/ Accessed October 21, 2019.

p. 46, "tired of the hypocrisy…" Ibid.

p. 48, "Where sound is concerned…" Lori Sealy, "What Does Autism Feel Like?" The Mighty, April 21, 2016, https://themighty.com/2016/04/what-does-autism-feel-like/ Accessed March 6, 2020.

p. 52/53, "One of the hardest…" Naomi Ondrasek, personal interview, October 25, 2019.

p. 55, "Don't be afraid to…" Jesse Shanahan, email to the author, October 25, 2019.

Select Bibliography

"Evelyn Glennie," Polar Music Prize, Nd, https://www.polarmusicprize.org/laureates/evelyn-glennie/ Accessed on October 17, 2019.

"Frida Kahlo: Appearances Can Be Deceiving," Brooklyn Museum, Nd, https://www.brooklynmuseum.org/exhibitions/frida_kahlo Accessed on February 24, 2020.

"Helen Keller Biography," American Foundation for the Blind, Nd, https://www.afb.org/about-afb/history/helen-keller/biography-and-chronology/biography Accessed on February 24, 2020.

Izadi, Elahe, "The Legacy of Stella Young, Disability Advocate and Comedian," *Washington Post*, December 8, 2014, https://www.washingtonpost.com/news/arts-and-entertainment/wp/2014/12/08/the-legacy-of-stella-young-australian-disability-advocate-and-comedian/ Accessed on October 18, 2019.

"Jaipur Foot: The Low-Cost Prosthetic that Revolutionised Medical Care in India and Beyond," Science Museum, November 28, 2017, https://blog.sciencemuseum.org.uk/jaipur-foot-the-low-cost-prosthetic-that-revolutionised-medical-care-in-india-and-beyond/ Accessed on February 24, 2020.

Matlin, Marlee, "Oscars: Marlee Matlin on Her Best Actress Win," *Entertainment Weekly*, February 21, 2012, https://ew.com/article/2012/02/21/oscars-marlee-matlin/ Accessed on October 10, 2019.

Pidd, Helen, "Trailblazer Zahra Nemati Wins Hearts and Minds with Stirring Effort in Archery," *The Guardian*, August 9, 2016, https://www.theguardian.com/sport/2016/aug/09/zahra-nemati-olympics-heart-and-minds-archery Accessed on February 24, 2020.

Salmon, Jacqueline L., "Kay Redfield Jamison: A Profile in Courage," BP Hope, Winter 2009, https://www.bphope.com/kay-redfield-jamison-a-profile-in-courage/ Accessed on October 21, 2019.

Sutton Williams, Natasha, "Sarah Gordy: 'I Wasn't Looking for a Professional Acting Career. It Found Me,'" *The Stage*, July 2, 2019, https://www.thestage.co.uk/features/interviews/2019/sarah-gordy-professional-acting-career/ Accessed on October 8, 2019.

Tripney Natasha, "Touretteshero's Jess Thom: 'Disabled People Need to Be Written In, Not Out,'" *The Stage*, February 28, 2018, https://www.thestage.co.uk/features/interviews/2018/tourettesheros-jess-thom-interview-disabled-people-need-to-written-in-not-out/ Accessed on October 14, 2019.

Wade, Alison, "Retired Pro Marla Runyan Continues to Inspire," *Runner's World*, October 1, 2014, https://www.runnersworld.com/races-places/a20820064/retired-pro-marla-runyan-continues-to-inspire/ Accessed on February 24, 2020.

"Wendy Fryke," PBS: Medal Quest, Nd, https://www.pbs.org/wgbh/medal-quest/athletes/detail/wendy-fryke/ Accessed on February 24, 2020.

About the Author

Emma Carlson Berne is the author of many books of historical nonfiction and biography for children and young adults. She lives in Cincinnati with her husband and three little boys.

Index